W9-DAT-721

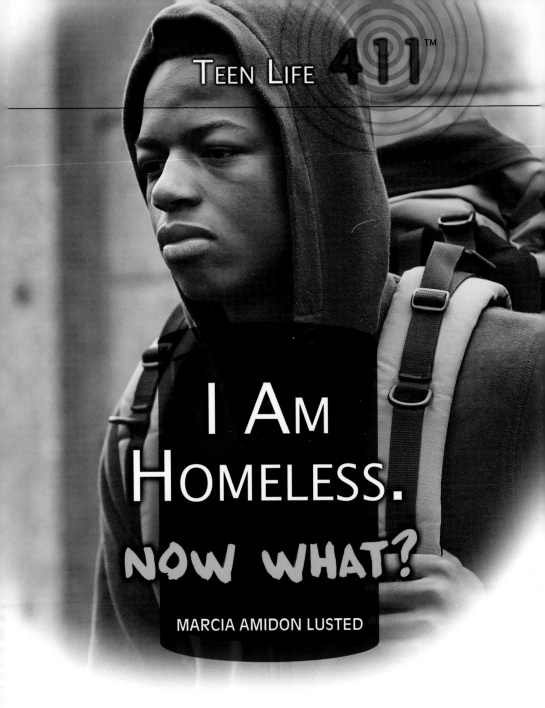

TEEN LIFE 411™

I AM HOMELESS.

NOW WHAT?

MARCIA AMIDON LUSTED

ROSEN
PUBLISHING®

New York

Published in 2017 by The Rosen Publishing Group, Inc.
29 East 21st Street, New York, NY 10010

Library of Congress Cataloging-in-Publication Data

Names: Lusted, Marcia Amidon, author.
Title: I am homeless. Now what? / Marcia Amidon Lusted.
Description: First edition. | New York : Rosen Publishing, 2017. | Series: Teen life 411 | Includes bibliographical references and index.
Identifiers: LCCN 2016017420 | ISBN 9781508171874 (library bound)
Subjects: LCSH: Homelessness—United States—Juvenile literature. | Homeless teenagers—United States—Juvenile literature. | Homeless persons—Services for—United States—Juvenile literature.
Classification: LCC HV4505 .L87 2017 | DDC 362.7/7569200830973—dc23
LC record available at https://lccn.loc.gov/2016017420

Manufactured in Malaysia

CONTENTS

When he first arrived in San Francisco, seventeen-year-old George slept in a tree in Golden Gate Park because he had nowhere to stay. He didn't expect to be homeless.

He had traveled to California after being told by his aunt that he had relatives in San Francisco with whom he could stay. When George arrived in the city, he learned that the address his aunt had given him was actually for a McDonald's restaurant, and his aunt admitted that he didn't have any relatives there. George was far away from his home in Missouri, with only $50 in his pocket and no place to stay or way to get home again. He was now officially homeless. George slept in the tree because it was safer than sleeping on the ground. "The only bad thing that could happen in a tree is if you fell out," he said. He washed himself with paper towels in a public restroom. He ate very little to save his money. He tried contacting his family. "I tried to call them twice and they didn't answer both times. Then I was like, 'What's the use?'" he said, in a report to ABC News.

George found himself as just one of the approximately two million homeless teens in the United States. His story has a happy ending, because he found a place at a shelter, finished high school, and then attended a community college. But his story is too common. Teens are especially vulnerable to becoming homeless. They might be kicked out of their homes because they don't get along with parents or other family members. They run away. Or when their families fall victim to bad economic circumstances, they are simply left with no place to go.

Homelessness is officially defined by the McKinney-Vento Homeless Assistance Act as "lacking housing," which includes people who are living in transitional shelters or doubled up with friends in their housing. It is no longer an unusual situation, especially after an

Many teens find themselves homeless because their families can no longer support them. They have no choice except to live on the streets.

It isn't always easy to tell if someone is homeless, but statistics show that there are many homeless teens all over the country.

extended period of economic downturns from which the United States has just started recovering. Families don't have the safety nets that they once did, and the tough transition from bad times to good times is happening too slowly to rescue them. Some families simply don't have any resources left and are forced to split up and leave their teenage children to fend for themselves.

Many smart, ambitious teens have suddenly found themselves yanked out of home and school through no fault of their own and forced to make their own way on the streets.

In short, homelessness is nothing to be ashamed or embarrassed about. It does not mean that you are stupid, or bad, or not as good as everyone else. There are millions of teens in the very same situation, all over the country. And while the situation is incredibly frightening, distressing, and even disorienting, especially if you've always had a safe, secure home, there are many resources out there for you if you suddenly find yourself to be homeless. You aren't alone, even if it feels like it. There are people and places ready to help you with shelter, food, psychological support, and school. You just need to know where to start.

CHAPTER 1

Just how widespread a problem is homelessness today, and what does it really mean? According to the National Alliance to End Homelessness's "State of Homelessness in America 2015":

> On a single night in January 2014, 578,424 people were experiencing homelessness—meaning they were sleeping outside or in an emergency shelter or transitional housing program. From 2013 to 2014, a period of ongoing recovery from the Great Recession, overall homelessness decreased by 2.3 percent and homelessness decreased among every major subpopulation: unsheltered persons (10 percent), families (2.7 percent), chronically homeless individuals (2.5 percent), and veterans (10.5 percent).

On paper, the outlook might start looking encouraging, but the hard truth on the streets is that almost 40 percent of homeless people in the United States are under the age of eighteen, and 34 percent are under the age of twenty-four. The Department of Justice estimates that

IT'S NOT A NEW THING

It may seem like homeless teens are an issue that we've only been talking about for twenty years. But during the 1930s and the Great Depression in America, homeless teens were a common sight.

Whether they had been forced to leave home because of the economic situation there, or simply decided it was a good time to chase freedom, many teens wandered the country as hoboes, as covered in McKenna Tucker's "Rail Riders" article. They hitched illegal rides on freight trains, frequently encountering violence and being injured or even killed. They faced hunger, poverty, constant danger, illness, and discrimination. But many parents who could not afford to feed their children would tell their teens to leave. "I wanted to stay home and fight that poverty with the family," said Clarence Lee, who was sixteen when he left home, "but my father told me I had to leave…he meant I had to go…I didn't have it in my mind to leave until he told me, 'Go fend for yourself. I cannot afford to have you around any longer.'" Teens who left simply to find the romance and adventure of travel found themselves struggling simply to survive.

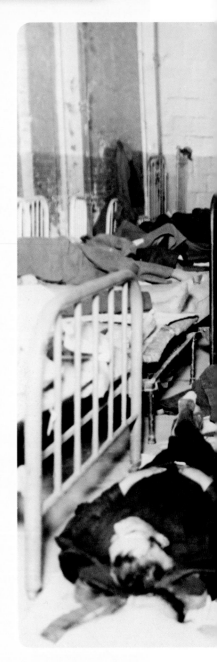

During the economic hardships of the Great Depression, teens were among the many homeless people looking for any place to sleep.

Some homeless families are able to find temporary housing in shelters, but there may be very little privacy.

every year, over 1.7 million teens in America will experience homelessness.

WHAT IS HOMELESSNESS?

What does it really mean to be homeless? Green Doors shares the official definition from the Department of Housing and Urban Development (HUD), and it's a bit complicated:

• People who are living in a place not meant for human habitation, in emergency shelter, in transitional housing, or are exiting an institution where they temporarily resided.
• People who are losing their primary nighttime residence, which may include a motel or hotel or a doubled-up

situation, within fourteen days and lack resources or support networks to remain in housing.

• Families with children or unaccompanied youth who are unstably housed and likely to continue in that state.

• People who are fleeing or attempting to flee domestic violence, have no other residence, and lack the resources or support networks to obtain other permanent housing.

In other words, the definition of homelessness isn't strictly limited to someone sleeping on the street.

It includes couch surfing with friends, or doubling up by sharing a room or apartment being rented by a friend of family member, even if you're not supposed to be there according to the lease or rental

Being able to stay together as a family unit can be the most difficult part of being homeless at times. Finding room for everyone is a major concern.

Some teens may end up being homeless when they have been released from a correctional institution or medical facility and have nowhere to go.

agreement. It might mean crashing in your friend's dorm room and sneaking food from their dining hall. It might mean moving in with a member of your extended family, like an aunt or grandparent or second cousin, or family friends who aren't related to you. It also includes living in a motel, rooming house, shelter, or even in your car. And then there are the homeless teens who live in abandoned buildings and other places not meant to be lived in, but which provide shelter when there isn't anything else to be found. These might include public parks, a bus or train station, a subway platform, an airport, or a campground.

Karen, whose story is told on the Covenant House website, was a teen who never expected to find herself homeless:

No one in her neat, quiet, suburban neighborhood would have thought the 15-year-old girl walking down the street had just been kicked out of her house. It was a freezing night and Karen had nowhere to go after her mother told her to get out. Exhausted and desperate for warmth, Karen stayed with friends for a few days. "You worry about freezing to death. You worry about being robbed and beaten up... about where you're going to get something to eat." No one chooses to be homeless, especially not a naive, 15-year-old girl. It's terrifying. Karen spent many nights wandering the streets for hours, trying to find a way to stay warm in the bitter cold. "Finding grates is the big thing," said Karen. The best she could do was to sleep on a grate— hoping the warm air would prevent her from freezing to death.

Homeless Families

Younger kids have their own category of homelessness, "children living in homeless families." Since they can't live on their own, they are homeless because their families are homeless. Perhaps their parents were evicted from their apartment, or their house was foreclosed on, so the entire family has gone to a homeless shelter or moved in with relatives. Green Doors has the stats on homeless families:

- Homeless families comprise roughly 34 percent of the total US homeless population.
- Approximately 1.6 million children will experience homelessness over the course of a year. In any given day, researchers estimate that more than two hundred thousand children have no place to live.
- People counted in the single adult homeless population (about 2.3-3.5 million annually) are also part of families:
  o Among all homeless women, 60 percent have children under age eighteen, but only 65 percent of them live with at least one of their children.
  o Among all homeless men, 41 percent have children under age eighteen, but only 7 percent live with at least one of their children.

HOMELESS TEENS

Homeless teens get their own designation: they are "unaccompanied youth." This basically means that they aren't living with their parents, are not in the foster care system, and do not live in an institution. Foster care is a program that places children with other adults or families when their own parents cannot care for them and is usually arranged by a court or a social services organization. An institution generally refers to a shelter, a hospital or treatment facility, transitional housing, a rehab facility, or even a correctional facility like a juvenile jail. A homeless teen doesn't have any of these options.

Kathy is an example from Covenant House of a homeless teen who came through the foster care system and ended up being homeless before finding a shelter:

Kathy came through our door...clutching a small paint can to her chest...One day, a concerned staff member approached Kathy...: "Kathy, that's a really nice can. What's in it?" For a long time, Kathy didn't answer...Then she looked over at the counselor with tears in her eyes and said: "This can belongs to me. It's my mother. It's my mother's ashes. I went and got them from the funeral home. See, it even has her name on it." Then Kathy held the can close, and hugged it. "I never really knew my mother...she threw me in the garbage two days after I was born. I ended up living in a lot of foster homes, mad at my mother," Kathy said. "But then, I decided I was going to try to find her. My mother was in the hospital. She had AIDS... I got to meet her the day before she died."

We know what homelessness is by definition, and through stories from teens who have been homeless, we can also know what homelessness *really* is and *really* feels like. But aside from statistics and reasons developed by government agencies and community organizations, what are the real, hard reasons why thousands upon thousands of teens end up homeless in the United States every year? You may find familiar stories

MYTHS AND FACTS

MYTH

The definition of a homeless person is someone living on the streets.

FACT

A homeless person may also be doubling up at a friend's house, living in a motel or shelter, or sleeping in their car.

MYTH

Homeless teens are all runaways.

FACT

Many teens become homeless because their families have forced them out of their home, often for economic reasons.

MYTH

It's easy to tell if a teen in your school is homeless.

FACT

Homeless teens are usually ashamed or embarrassed to be homeless. They will try to look as normal as possible so that no one knows.

in the hard facts of teen homelessness, either in your own life, the life of a friend, or classmate.

You may also find a thread in the causes of homelessness that will make you aware of circumstances in your own life—or again, a friend's—that make you or them vulnerable to becoming homeless, too.

CHAPTER 2

HOW DID I GET TO BE HOMELESS?

We know what homelessness is, and that it isn't always just finding yourself on the streets with no place to take shelter and no resources to fall back on. In actuality, it is the lack of a permanent home, somewhere where you are safe and warm and fed, can go to school and focus on learning without more than the usual distractions, and don't have to worry about where you'll sleep that night or how you can get something to eat.

HOW DO FAMILIES BECOME HOMELESS?

In talking about homelessness and its causes, it's simplest to start with the category of "children living in homeless families." Why do families become homeless? There are many reasons noted by the National Coalition for the Homeless. One became more and more common during the economic downturn that took place roughly between 2007 and 2010, from which many people in America have not yet recovered.

Many homes were foreclosed on in 2008 when their owners could
no longer afford to pay their mortgages. Many of these were families
that became homeless.

HURRICANE KATRINA

One clear example of how a natural disaster can create homelessness is that of Hurricane Katrina, which hit New Orleans, Louisiana, in 2005. Over a million people along the Gulf Coast were displaced from their homes. Bill Quigley and Sara H. Godchaux reported that many of the affordable housing projects in New Orleans had to be demolished because of flood damage and were not rebuilt. About 150,000 houses and apartment units were destroyed by the hurricane, and 79 percent of it was affordable or low-income housing. Even people who owned their homes saw them condemned as unfit to live in because of damage, and those owners couldn't always afford the repairs. As a result of Katrina, many families lost their homes, and many simply left the area permanently.

Hurricane Katrina earned New Orleans national headlines, both because of the severity of the damage and the problems with the evacuation and clean-up afterward.

Families may be spending much of their income to live in unsafe, unsanitary rental properties because it's all they can afford.

Many people who were given subprime mortgages to finance buying a home beyond their means found themselves foreclosed on, which means that they couldn't afford to pay their mortgages. The banks took back their houses when they didn't meet their payments, forcing those families to become homeless. Between 2008 and 2009 alone, the number of foreclosures jumped by 34 percent. That not only meant that people who had bought homes were evicted. It also meant that people who rented homes from owners who were foreclosed on also were evicted.

Family homelessness is often tightly linked to

poverty. After all, if a family only has a certain amount of money to use for housing, food, childcare, health care, and everything else that a family needs, they have to choose where to spend that money. According to Matthew Desmond, author of *Evicted: Poverty and Profit in the American City*, housing takes up a much higher percentage of a family's income than anything else. One in five renters in the United States is spending half his or her income on a place to live. It's even worse in inner cities where rents are very high, and it can take 70 percent of a family's income just to rent an apartment. According to the US Census Bureau, in 2014 there were 46.7 million Americans living in poverty, a rate of 14.8 percent of the total population. For children under eighteen, the poverty rate was 21 percent. This makes for a large number of people who become homeless simply because they can't afford a place to live.

The National Coalition for the Homeless cites several reasons for homelessness. First of all, children and their families become homeless because of unemployment and fewer job opportunities. Many jobs no longer pay enough for a family to be able to afford housing. For workers who make only minimum wage at their job, they cannot afford even a one or two bedroom apartment. Many homeless people actually have jobs but still don't make enough to have a stable place to live. And when people lose their jobs, they often lose their homes or are evicted from rentals because they fall behind on payments. Eviction is also a stigma that continues long after leaving a particular rental property. Once a family has a record of being evicted, future landlords are reluctant to rent to them for fear that they will have to be evicted again.

Another reason why children and families become homeless is because there is less public assistance available for them. Programs that provide vouchers toward rent payments are difficult to get into because too many people need the service. People who are leaving the welfare system often have trouble finding jobs and housing because of low wages and the loss of government benefits. There is also a lack of affordable housing for families, depending on where they live. Families end up living in substandard housing, which is housing with conditions like bad plumbing, unsafe floors, dangerous wiring, and holes in windows and walls, simply because it's all they can afford or all that is available.

Finally, some personal factors can lead to homelessness. The family might consist of a single parent who can't pay all the bills alone. There can be abusive or criminal situations that make it impossible to remain in a home. A serious illness or disability might make it impossible to keep paying rent. Addiction can be a huge problem as well, especially if the primary wage earner is spending too much money on drugs or alcohol. And even if it doesn't happen frequently, a natural disaster such as a flood or severe storm can also destroy homes or make them unfit to be lived in.

CONTRIBUTING FACTORS TO TEEN HOMELESSNESS

So we know why many "children living in homeless families" get to be that way. But what are the reasons why teens arrive at the point of being "unaccompanied youth?" Absolute living-on-the-street homelessness is a much more desperate situation than moving to a relative's house or sleeping on a friend's porch, but there are circumstances that force teens to take such drastic action.

One of the biggest reasons why teens end up being homeless is physical or sexual abuse taking place in their home. It can be abuse at the hands of a parent, a sibling, a stepparent or stepsibling, or the boyfriend or girlfriend of a parent. Generally, the abuse gets to the

Sometimes, a desperate situation calls for desperate measures to be taken. However, going from one unsafe place to another without a plan may not be the right answer.

point where the teen can no longer stand it or is in fear for their life, so they have no choice but to leave and become homeless.

Covenant House tells the story of Jodie who found herself at a shelter after her mother abused her. Because her mother constantly told her she was stupid and worthless, Jodie had never learned to read or write:

> Her mother's callous words were often accompanied by violent blows to Jodie's head with a frying pan. These may have caused irreparable harm to Jodie's growing brain or compromised her ability to learn to read and write. Jodie also has terrible scarring on her right arm. "Usually she just smacked me on the head with the frying pan. But this one time she was so mad she took this big thing of hot oil she was frying something in and she just threw it at me." [Jodie] chose the uncertainty of homelessness over certain fear and violence at home. But being illiterate made it that much harder to survive alone. She was unable to decipher signs on buildings or read street names... [or] on a store shelf. No one would hire her... and Jodie's situation made her particularly vulnerable to the dangers that face all homeless kids.

Another reason why teens become homeless can be a result of a family member's addiction to alcohol or drugs. The National Resource Center on Domestic Violence notes that this can lead to abusive behavior toward the teen, or at least a generally dysfunctional family life. They might be neglected or maltreated, their medical records aren't kept current so they can't attend school because of required vaccinations, they might be left alone in the house to fend for themselves for long periods of time, or there is routine family violence, even if it isn't directed at them specifically. David Daniels, writing for the Children's Rights blog, recalls what it was like to live with addicted parents:

> I was born a "drug baby" and was placed into child protective services (CPS) immediately upon my arrival into this world. My parents were drug addicts, and my father abused me and my mother. Rewind, right? I know you're wondering how I was abused and witnessed my parents doing drugs if I was in foster care from birth. Well, when I was 5 years old I was returned home. My mother was drug-free, or so everyone thought. For years after, my father abused me and my mother neglected me. Sometimes I went days without bathing. I would miss school because of the bruises on my body. I was terrified of my father, and tired of being in crack houses with my mother.

Other influences that may lead teens to leave their families and become homeless are the desire for independence, especially if they are rebelling against punishments that seem harsh or are applied for very minor wrongdoings, and strained family relationships.

Teens often leave home to escape from abusive situations. Some may fear for their lives and others simply cannot take the abuse any longer.

This can often happen when a parent starts a new relationship with a new partner.

A noticeable factor in causing teens to run away and become homeless is their sexual identity. A huge percentage of homeless teens are lesbian, gay, transgender, bisexual, intersex, asexual, or questioning. Known by the initials LGBTQIA, it is estimated by the National Alliance to End Homelessness that 40 percent of homeless teens fall into this category. They include more African American, Native Americans, and teens from low-income households in this mix as well, and many cited "severe family conflict" over their sexuality as being the reason they left home. Once homeless, they are at higher risk for sexual abuse, mental health issues, and suicide.

Tank, who is gay, shared his experiences with the *Advocate* about being homeless in New York City:

> I grew up in Queens. I had to leave home because I was abused by my mother; called a faggot, vulgar stuff. When I was with friends who were also homeless, we would huddle together, sometimes in Union Square, sometimes in Staten Island. We would sleep in Staten Island in abandoned buildings that had been left wrecked by Hurricane Sandy. Once when we walked on the floor, the floorboard broke underneath us, and a friend had his leg split open. We closed the wound and took him out into the street before we called the ambulance. We didn't want anyone to know where we were staying. We were afraid to stay in the adult shelters—we heard too many things about LGBT kids being beaten and robbed there.

What other circumstances force teens out of their homes and onto the streets?

Many are situations where teens are made to leave instead of choosing to run away. They might have parents who live in extreme poverty and know that once their child is eighteen and legally an adult, they are no longer obliged to support them and can turn them out of the house. Or perhaps a parent's job loss or death makes the household dissolve. Perhaps the family's earnings or government benefits aren't high enough to support a teen family member who may or may not be a legal adult and may or may not be able to fend for themselves. This leads to situations where teens move out and get jobs, only to find that their wages aren't high enough for them to be able to afford their own housing. Another factor is when a teen leaves a situation like foster care or institutional care, doesn't have any home to return to, and can't find a place to live, notes the Homeless Hub.

Becoming homeless either on their own as part of their family can be extremely difficult for teens to handle, as it was for Scott, who shared his story with the Daily Kos:

> When the family lost their house, they moved into an RV parked on his uncle's driveway...Although Scott is an only child, he feels crowded and thinks of the Winnebago as a personal insult to him...Although his anger and frustration has not yet turned into law-breaking or being disruptive at school, Scott admits to smoking dope "a few times a week," undoubtedly a way of escaping the pain he feels. And what hurts him almost as much as being evicted from the house—where he had his own room—is that his many of his friends banished him from their circle when the family became homeless. "Like it was my fault or something," Scott says...All of the negatives in his life have caused Scott to withdraw, both at school and from his family.

Teen Runaways

Although not all teens become homeless because of family circumstances or other things beyond their control, most teens in the "unaccompanied youth" category are also runaways. The US Department of Housing and Urban Development (HUD) has created four terms to describe runaway and homeless youth:

• Throwaway youth: Youth who have been asked, told, or forced to leave home by parents or caregivers with no alternate care arranged.

• Runaway youth: Youth who have left home without parental/caregiver permission and stay away for one or more nights. A runaway episode has been defined as being away from home overnight for youth under fourteen (or older and mentally incompetent) and for two or more nights for youth fifteen and older. Research suggests that the experience of youth running away from home is often episodic rather than chronic with youth running away for short periods of time and returning home, in some cases multiple times.

• Street youth: Youth who have spent at least some time living on the streets without a parent or caregiver.

• Systems youth: Youth who become homeless after aging out of foster care or exiting the juvenile justice system.

So there are many, many different reasons why children and teens become homeless. But whether or not

1. What is the biggest reason why teens become homeless?

2. Do homeless teens have the right to stay in school?

3. What are the biggest risks that homeless teens face?

4. What should a teen do first if they become homeless?

5. What should a teen do first if they have a friend who becomes homeless?

6. What are the worst places to go when you're homeless?

7. What are the best places to go if you become homeless?

8. What organizations in this areas help homeless teens?

9. What are the biggest do's and don't's for home-less teens?

10. How many homeless teens are there in my area?

they choose to live on the streets, with a friend, in a shel-ter, or with a distant relative, teens must all face the same things that can happen to them when they become home-less. They range from health issues, to mental health problems, to education and safety, but they are all risks that homeless youth may face every single day.

CHAPTER 3

WHAT CAN HAPPEN TO ME IF I'M HOMELESS?

Being a teenager is tough, even when you live in a stable home with a loving family and attend school regularly. But if a teen is homeless, then the usual problems of being a teenager are magnified and even more complicated, and there are many other additional hazards. Pressures such as substance abuse and sex are even stronger. Being a teen is learning good decision-making skills and how to handle strong emotions, but when teens live on the streets, these processes can be blunted by the need to survive and the need to find some comfort or connection. It may also become necessary to trade sex for food or drugs. The truth is that being on the streets carries with it many perils, and homeless teens can easily end up suffering from serious health problems, can be taken advantage of, and may even die.

The National Child Traumatic Stress Network raises public awareness of all the dangers facing children and teens in tough situations. Joe's story is a common one for homeless teens and illustrates some of its hazards and consequences:

Joe is a 17-year-old...[he] was removed from his home when he was about five years old because his mother had a significant substance abuse problem and he had been physically abused by several of her boyfriends. Joe has lived in various foster care settings and group homes, but he got into fights with his peers and transferred frequently due to anger management problems. He ran away from the most recent group home because he said he didn't want to continue living with people who didn't really care about him. He thinks he has completed school up to the ninth grade, but it is hard to know, since he changed schools so often due to his various placements. He currently lives in a "squat"—an abandoned building—with a group of other homeless youth he calls his family. Joe panhandles for money and admits to shoplifting to get food.

So what are the things that can happen to a homeless teen, living on the streets? They fall into several major categories. There are mental health problems, substance abuse, criminal activity and victimization, unsafe sexual practices, physical health problems from lack of food and sleep, and obstacles to attending school or finding a job. And of course, there is the constant question of physical safety and the constant exposure to violence.

Living on the streets can make teens vulnerable to violence and abuse. Some engage in drugs and sex simply to dull the pain, find a connection, or make money.

MENTAL HEALTH

Mental health issues may seem like the least of a homeless teen's worries, when issues like finding something to eat and a safe place to stay are much more immediate. But these kinds of problems can lead to a host of other problems. They include major depression, acting out with inappropriate behavior or poor decision-making abilities, impulsiveness, stress, self-harm, suicidal behavior, and the shame and embarrassment of being homeless, which affects self-esteem. According to the National Network for Youth, mental health issues are as much as eleven times higher for home-less teens than for the general population. Out of all homeless teens, 32 percent have attempted suicide, and very few have access to or have used any mental health services.

Some mental health issues are a result of becoming homeless, while others were always there but untreated. In a story with the CBC, Sheila Harms, a youth psychologist describes it: "It's a really interesting question of the chicken or the egg. A lot of the young people I've been working with have pre-existing mental health issues that would have been identified in early childhood—learning disabilities, ADHD, acting-out behaviors. Over time, for whatever reason, the family system hasn't been able to contain them or provide the type of course that's needed," she said.

Being homeless can lead to escalation of mental issues. Lack of treatment options and the stress of being displaced make the daily struggles harder to bear.

HEALTH TO GO

Many homeless teens cannot receive help with their health problems because they have no access to traditional health care. They may not have health insurance or a regular doctor, and both doctor's offices and clinics may be located too far away to access without transportation. NPR reported on an organization designed to address these problems. In California, one approach has been the creation of a mobile Teen Health Van that is sponsored by Stanford University's children's hospital and the Children's Health Fund.

The van parks on streets in the San Francisco area where homeless teens are known to be, and offers free medical, mental health, and nutritional services, as well as reproductive health services and treatment for substance abuse and chronic health issues. "Going to the patients makes all the difference," says Dr. Seth Ammerman, "and it's not just a matter of convenience. It really is that these kids, because of all these access barriers—lack of insurance, lack of transportation— they're not going to get this kind of care unless we go to them."

In San Francisco, CA, the mobile teen health van brings health care services to teens who are homeless and have no access to regular health care. Young people are encouraged to approach these mobile health stations and seek help with any health concerns.

Leaving home, though, doesn't necessarily fix their problems. "If every day you're looking for food, you're looking for a safe place to live, a lot of people struggle with their mental health. Kids are scared. Kids are forced to do all kinds of things to survive. And that contributes to mental illness."

PHYSICAL HEALTH

In addition to mental health issues, which can lead to behaviors like poor judgment and inappropriate sexual encounters as well as substance abuse, there is the very real risk to physical health. If you're sleeping on the streets and not getting enough to eat, your body is going to suffer. In cold weather there is the risk of exposure and frostbite. Common illnesses like colds can deteriorate into something worse through a poor environment and lack of access to even basic medicines like pain killers or antihistamines.

The HRSA Health Service program details the risks homeless teens face to their wellbeing. More serious conditions go untreated and unmedicated because of lack of access to doctors and health care. Poor nutrition can lead to either obesity or being too thin, as well as making the body more vulnerable to illnesses. Teeth can suffer as a result, too. Even shelters and soup kitchens may not be serving food with the appropriate level of nutrients in it, especially fruits, vegetables, and dairy products. And if you're living in a dirty environment without adequate access to soap and water, even a small cut can become infected and cause major problems. For girls, lack of access to regular health care and birth control can result in unwanted pregnancies. Both boys and girls are at risk for sexually transmitted diseases, too, including HIV.

SUBSTANCE ABUSE

Substance abuse can be a huge problem for homeless teens, because it's a way to cope with a terrible situation and handle stress and deprivation. According to the National Network for Youth [NN4Y], homeless teens are three times more likely to smoke pot and eighteen times more likely to use crack cocaine than the average teen. And in many parts of the country, heroin use is skyrocketing, too. Out of all homeless teens, 30 to 40 percent report problems with alcohol abuse, and 40 to 50 percent have drug problems. Very few of them are ever treated for their substance abuse problems.

Sarah Lyon was a typical teenager living in suburban Chicago, until she had an argument with her mother and was kicked out of her house. She had nowhere to go and ended up living on the street. The *Chicago Tribune* covered her story:

Struggling with a heroin addiction, Lyon began living in abandoned buildings on Chicago's West Side, where she bought her drugs. After roughly five years on the streets, Lyon, now 24, said she has become somewhat jaded after a number of harrowing experiences, including multiple arrests, being approached by a pimp and being robbed at gunpoint—twice. "I had $60 on me, and I was going with some other people looking for drugs late at night," said Lyon, recalling the last time she was robbed. "The guy said he was going to get it and he pulled a gun out—a big (expletive) gun. He said, 'Give me everything you have.' I said, 'No problem.' "I was scared, but you're so numb because of everything going on."

Now Sarah and her boyfriend sleep on the steps of a monument in one of the city's squares, and

Being homeless can make teens vulnerable to a lot of dangers, especially when coming from sheltered backgrounds.

A homeless teen with no place to sleep on a freezing night may resort to breaking into empty buildings to find shelter.

panhandle every day to get the $40 they need for their heroin habits. In the winter they find shelter in abandoned houses.

CRIMINAL ACTIVITY

Living on the streets means living in a constant state of desperation, and that often leads homeless teens to criminal activity or to being the victims of crimes. If you have no place to sleep on a freezing cold night, you might break into an empty house for shelter. The National Network for Youth reports that many homeless teens—14 percent— admit to breaking into a house. Many others are forced to steal, especially shoplifting food and clothing. Out of all homeless teens, 25 percent report having carried out some kind of theft.

If you're desperate for money, then becoming involved in prostitution or selling drugs might be the only survival strategy you have. Gang membership might be a kind of safety, but often it also means participating in criminal activities. Homeless teens are frequently arrested by police, sometimes because they have no other way to help these teens and can at least offer a half-solution within the criminal justice system, which will provide them with shelter and food, even if just temporarily.

More often, however, homeless teens are on the receiving end of criminal activity. They are often raped or assaulted or robbed. The NN4Y notes that the likelihood of being assaulted or raped when you're a homeless teen is two to three times higher than for teens with regular homes. The chances of sexual assault are greater for females and for LGBTQIA teens. And many homeless teens will experience posttraumatic stress disorder (PTSD) as a result of their exposure to crime and violence on the streets.

Unsafe Sex

In addition to increased chances of being sexually assaulted, many homeless teens find themselves involved with unsafe practices when it comes to consensual sex. They might be involved in survival sex, which simply means exchanging sex for money, food, shelter, or other necessities. They may become prostitutes, managed by a pimp who sells their services without giving them all of the money that is paid for those services. And there are, of course, homeless teens who have sex simply because they want the companionship and caring of a relationship, even temporarily.

No matter what the reason for it, almost all homeless teens—a reported 95 percent—claim to be sexually active, although most say they only engage in survival sex when they're homeless. The average age for becoming sexually active on the streets is thirteen. Pregnancy is a very high risk, as a result, especially with no stable housing or access to birth control, and as many as 50 percent of teens living on the streets have had a pregnancy, or at least a "pregnancy experience" for those who haven't actually been pregnant but have been involved with a pregnancy.

Some homeless teens don't even seem to believe that birth control is important, and they don't have access to information about sexual health and safety. The NN4Y notes that HIV, AIDS, and other STDs are a huge problem, especially since most educational programs about sexually transmitted diseases are targeted at teens in school, a place that many homeless teens can no longer attend.

All of these things can happen to homeless teens, and do. The physical and mental health aspects are pretty dire, and health issues and the exposure to violence can ultimately cause death. Dr. Natasha Slesnick from the University of Ohio warns that homeless teens are twelve times more likely to die than teens with stable homes. The most common causes are untreated illnesses, assaults, and suicide.

DROPPING OUT OF SCHOOL

While the biggest hazards associated with being a homeless teen are very real in terms of basic survival, there are other effects of homelessness that can last a lifetime. First, there are barriers to receiving a good education. Homeless teens often drop out of school and never finish high school, simply because they can no longer attend school because it's too far away, or they are more concerned with survival.

If you have no place to do your homework, no place to shower and no clean clothes, and not enough

With no safe place to live, not enough food or sleep, and no way to do homework, many homeless teens find it difficult to stay in school.

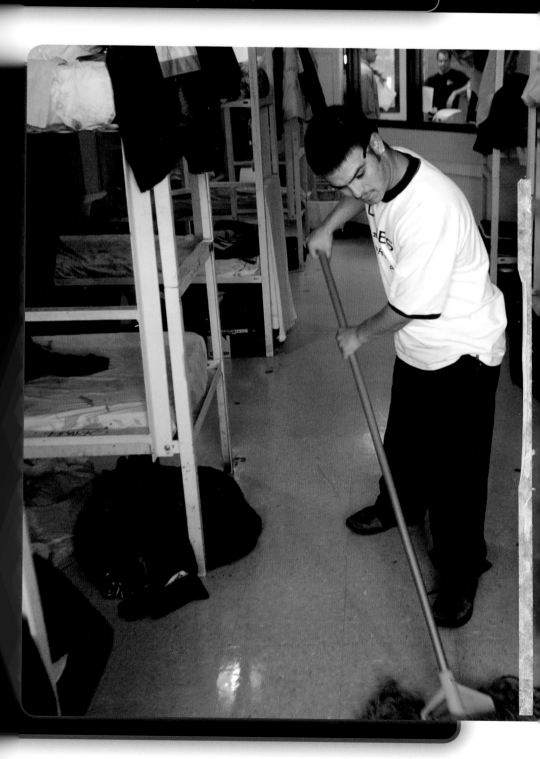

When the daily struggle to find a place to sleep and something to eat is the biggest concern, school might feel like a much lower priority to a homeless teenager.

to eat, then you're not likely to be able to study for a test, write a paper, or show up every day ready to learn.

It also does not help that teens can "age out" of the foster care system (meaning that they become too old for the social services system) at seventeen, often leaving them homeless before they've graduated from high school. A homeless teen is 87 percent more likely to drop out of school than a student with stable housing , according to Alexandra Pannoni in the *U.S. News & World Report*.

Mandy, a high school drop-out, described her reasons on Gradnation.org for leaving school:

When I turned eighteen I [aged out of foster care] and

became homeless and that's where it all started. It just went downhill. I withdrew myself [from school] because I had nowhere to go. I was staying in tunnels, under highways, and deserts. I withdrew myself so that way I didn't have to worry about that and survival. I didn't have time to go and make what I needed for food and go to school at the same time. It don't work that way. You can't do both.

Dropping out of high school also means dropping out of the normal socialization and maturing of high school teens, too, which can impact a teen's ability to live independently in the future.

LIMITED JOB PROSPECTS

Lack of education, coupled with the lack of a permanent address and shelter, also makes it very difficult to get a job if you're a homeless teen. Finding a job in today's economy can be tough even with a high school degree, so not having one is a serious barrier to anything but the lowest-paid jobs. Even getting a job at a fast food restaurant can be difficult with no home address or phone for contact information or for arranging interviews. And not having the education and skills for the job market will eventually hurt society as a whole, since there will be a shortage of trained, educated young people to take over for workers who retire.

In short, there are many, many things that can happen to you when you become a homeless teen. They can hurt your physical and mental health, affect your ability to go to school or get a job, and even put you at risk of serious injury or death. And yet many of these things might seem unavoidable if you are to survive on the streets. One thing that can help you, if you suddenly find yourself homeless, is to know what to do and where to find the resources that can help you.

CHAPTER 4

WHERE TO GO for HELP

So you're suddenly homeless. What is it like to face that first night alone, on the street? Mark Horvath recounted his first night alone for the Huffington Post:

I'll never forget my first night. All of a sudden…I found myself homeless in Koreatown near downtown Los Angeles. I was sober, but I had no money, no place to go and no one I could call for help. I was officially homeless…I walked 11 or so miles [17 kilometers] to the valley. By the time I arrived, it was beginning to get dark, so I started to think about where I was going to sleep. I decided to try a park…But when I arrived, I noticed gang members hanging around in the dark, so…I continued walking to park after park. I just didn't feel safe in any of them. My feet were becoming swollen; I was emotionally and physically exhausted. I knew that the worst crimes… happened at night to people living outdoors. I knew that when you sleep outside, you are vulnerable to just about everything. I was scared.

You might be homeless out of a desperate choice, running away from home because of violence or abuse. Or you might find yourself homeless by other circumstances, such as being told to leave by your parents. Either way, being on the street is a disorienting and frightening feeling.

Where can you go? Who can you contact? Is there someplace or someone who can help you? The blog Guide2Homelessness and Venture Article's "What to Do When You're Homeless" are full of suggestions expanded on in this chapter.

WHERE CAN I STAY?

Most teens will begin by trying to find a place to stay with some other family member, such as an adult sibling, grandparents, or aunts and uncles. This is probably the best place to start, since they are your family and hopefully are more sympathetic to your situation and helping you.

Some teens call their friends, and this can work for a few nights. Most friends, however, probably have families who, unless they are really concerned and caring, won't look fondly at having a new, unrelated family member for an indefinite period of time. Some may be concerned about the legal implications of letting you stay at their house for a long time. And just because you are staying with a relative or your close friend, this doesn't guarantee that those places are totally safe for you. There may be situations and relationships there that are potentially abusive or violent, too.

The first thing to do is to find help from organizations and services that are intended to help homeless teens. If you are still in high school, start with your school guidance counselor or even the school nurse or a trusted teacher. Explain what has happened and that you have nowhere to go. Chance are there are already procedures in place that allow the school to help you. If there aren't, you're still likely to find adults who can help you or, in a pinch, take you in.

If you can't find temporary shelter with a family member, friend, or through school, it would be a good time to call a runaway or homeless hotline for teens,

A teen's first few days of homelessness can be an extremely frightening experience, with no idea of where to go for help.

Volunteers who answer phones at homeless hotlines are trained to help teens who are frightened and don't know what to do. They can provide information and help.

Keeping America's runaway and at-risk youth safe and off the streets.

1-800-RUNAWAY
www.1800RUNAWAY.org

one that has information about resources and places where you can go. These hotlines are available twenty-four hours a day. The people who answer those phones are well-trained in how to deal with desperate and frightened homeless teens, and can not only help you find what you need, but calm you down and be a sympathetic ear as well.

They include the National Runaway Safeline (1-800-RUNAWAY), and National Safe Place, a project of the YMCA, has a program called TEXT4HELP which allows you to text the word SAFE and your location to 69866. Within seconds, you will receive a message with the closest Safe

Place location and contact number for the local youth shelter. You will also have the option to text interactively with a mental health professional for more help. There are many more hotlines that operate locally and can provide you with local shelters and other resources.

Another place to look for help is a church or other religious organization, whether it's your own church or not. Some churches have facilities or even funds for helping people in need, such as soup kitchens or shelters, or simply a way to provide money for a few nights' refuge.

The religious leader of the church might also have connections and be able to offer help. It depends on where you are and if your area has a large number of homeless people. If it does, there are more likely to be church programs and outreaches available for newly homeless teens.

City and state agencies can help as well. If you feel that you're in danger, go to your local police station and ask them for help. They will have access to city and state organizations that can help. Also, many national organizations have offices in many cities and already have systems in place to help the homeless. This includes Goodwill, which actually operates shelters in some cities, the YMCA/YWCA, and the Salvation Army. The US Department of Housing and Urban Development (HUD) also has a Homelessness Assistance web page with a locator tool for finding resources in your specific area.

There are usually homeless shelters that you can try for immediate help to get off the streets. Covenant House is an organization dedicated to homeless youth, with shelters all over the country, as well as services. They offer protection from life on the street, a sense of security, and help to build a positive future.

It is extremely important to always start with legitimate organizations and government and agency sources for help in finding shelter, which is generally the very first thing a homeless teen thinks about. Options like living in your car, staying at a campground, staying at a youth hostel or a hotel, or staying in a public place like a library, train station, or subway station should always be a last resort. The chances of being abused, robbed, assaulted, or suffering physical harm are much greater in these kinds of places. They should only be used if there is absolutely no other option.

"What to Do When You're Homeless" is a good checklist of information, especially regarding your material possessions. Remember that your possessions can be difficult to deal with when you're on the move or in a shelter. Ideally, find a safe place to leave them with a family member or a friend. Even if these people aren't able to offer you shelter, they might be willing to store your belongings for a while. You may also end up selling some of the things you don't need and using that money to live on. But no matter where you're staying, in a shelter or on the street, you are vulnerable to theft, so try not to keep anything with you that you don't actually need and can't risk losing.

I'M HUNGRY

Once you have found a place to stay, the next greatest need is for food. If you are staying at a shelter, you will also be able to eat meals there, which is a great help. If you are still able to attend school, ask your principal about free breakfasts and lunches in the cafeteria. These are generally available depending on family income, and if you have no income, then you are certainly eligible.

Another option is to find a local soup kitchen, which is the term used for places that provide free meals to those in need. While it may feel embarrassing at first to ask about and find a soup

Soup kitchens, church groups, and homeless shelters often provide free meals for homeless people.

kitchen, the staff and volunteers that run them are almost always highly empathetic.

Some soup kitchens are run by state agencies, some are sponsored by churches, and others are private facilities started by concerned individuals or community groups. They are a good place to get a hot meal and often also have connections to other agencies that can help the homeless. They might require you to help in the kitchen or with cleanup as the "price" of your meal, but it's generally not difficult work.

If you have access to a kitchen or some other way to cook food, you can visit a food pantry. Again, these are usually run by churches, community groups, or state agencies, and their hours of operation may vary. They can generally supply you with a bag of free groceries. The best way to find these places can be to Google "food for homeless" and pull up results in your area. If you don't have access to a computer, you can use free internet access and computers at a library to find the information. Remember, too, that if you have a low income or no place to stay, you are probably eligible for food stamps from the government. Visit the local office of social services and they can help you apply for these, or visit the government's website for food stamps.

Your very last option is to ask local restaurants, bakeries, or grocery stores if you can have their unsold food at the end of the day. Some places will allow this, but it depends on their regulations. You should never eat food from restaurant or grocery store dumpsters, however, since it may be contaminated or spoiled and can cause serious health issues.

PERSONAL HYGIENE

How do you stay clean when you're homeless? Shelters usually have good bathroom and shower facilities, but you may not have that option. The next best option is to find public restrooms, especially in large chain stores where you will be less obvious. You can use their sinks to wash up, but if you need to take a sponge bath or a shower, look for public places where showers are provided, such as a pool, park, or even a school locker room.

Some hospitals have accessible rest rooms with showers as well. Lake or ocean swimming areas usually have showers, as well as campsites. Using a lake or a river for washing up is not recommended, since there is no privacy and the water may be of questionable quality.

For clean clothes, you can wash things out in the sink of a public restroom, or if you have some money, use a Laundromat. School gyms often have washing machines and dryers as well, for washing sports uniforms, and you might be able to use those.

One important thing that you should try very hard to hold on to is your cell phone. You can use it to find help in an emergency, such as an injury or an assault. It can be vital for finding resources for the homeless, for maintaining contact with your family and friends, and especially if you apply for a job. If no one can

Peer counselors can be a valuable asset when it comes to finding employment and support to get yourself off the streets.

reach you, it's hard to get a job interview. If your cell phone service has been disconnected, you can buy a pay-as-you-go cell phone and use that.

ADDRESSING MEDICAL CONCERNS

Medical care can also be difficult to find when you're homeless. Most hospitals and emergency clinics have to treat you if you are hurt or seriously ill, even if you don't have insurance, but they aren't an option for regular health care. There are usually organizations that provide reduced cost or free medical care, and you can either Google these or ask about them at the local hospital or other care facility. These are often state run. Some communities have outreach clinics in areas where homeless people are most likely to live or mobile clinics that travel to certain areas at certain times.

How Can I Start Earning Money?

With a place to stay and food to eat, you may be able to turn your attention to finding a job. Job searching is the same for homeless teens as it is for teens with regular housing, but it will be more difficult if you can't seek employment wearing clean clothes and providing a contact address and phone number and references.

If it seems totally impossible to get a job, then there are some small sources of income such as collecting and recycling aluminum cans in states where there is a law for bottle and can deposits. If you still have a computer and can find a place with internet access, you might also be able to find internet jobs that pay, such as writing articles and other content.

These may take a while to earn you any real money, and you will need to have a bank account for automatic deposits.

Traditional jobs for teens, such as babysitting and lawn mowing, may be out of reach for homeless teens, but if you knew a family with children or did yard work for a neighbor before you became homeless, they know you and might still be willing to pay you. Shelters and other homeless resources can also help you continue

The US Department of Housing and Urban Development (HUD) has established several initiatives for home-less youth. One is intended specifically for LGBTQ homeless teens, and is called the Lesbian, Gay, Bisexual, Transgender, and Questioning (LGBTQ) Youth Homelessness Prevention Initiative. Its purpose is "to identify successful strategies to ensure that no young person is left without a home because of their sexual orientation or gender identity and expression. The initiative's plans include strategies to prevent LGBTQ youth from becoming homeless and intervene as early as possible if they do become homeless." HUD also has the Youth Count! and Rapid Rehousing initiatives for home-less teens, designed to help communities understand their population of homeless teens and to quickly find housing for teens who become homeless.

INITIATIVES

your education and find employment. There are also places that will employ you temporarily with an eye to offering you a permanent job if they like your work and you are dependable.

FOCUS ON A SOLUTION

At the end of the day, your biggest task is to get back on your feet. Many teens think that shelters can be restrictive—especially if they left home because they didn't want to follow strict rules and regulations from their parents—but they can also offer a place to stay and the opportunity to finish high school, get a job, and find your own housing. You may also be able to get a scholarship for college. Most cities also have job placement services and housing assistance for low income workers.

If you find that you cannot return home, then the best way out of homelessness, and to staying safe while you do it, is through a shelter or organizations that are intended to help homeless teens. There are many, many successful people in the world who endured periods of homelessness and yet still managed to pull themselves out of it and find secure, satisfying lives. It will happen to you, too, if you are careful and open to opportunity.

CHAPTER 5

Perhaps you are one of the lucky ones: a teen who doesn't have to worry about homelessness and surviving on the street. You have a roof over your head, plenty of food and warm clothes, and the opportunity to go to school, get an education, and still have time for fun and friends. But you may have a homeless friend or have the desire to help homeless teens in your area. So what can you do?

WHAT TO LOOK FOR

Since one of the biggest reasons why teens become homeless is because they run away from home, there are some warning signs to be aware of in your friends and classmates. If your friend seems likely to run away, you can offer help and resources and perhaps prevent them from becoming homeless.

What are the warning signs that a teen might be getting ready to run away from home? The Miami Museum of Science has an excellent checklist you can consult:

- Communication problems with parents
- Conflicts with stepparents or a parent's new partner
- Withdrawing from friends
- Suicide or death of a relative or close friend
- Recent severe illness of someone in the family
- Loss of interest in personal appearance
- Using drugs or alcohol, or using them more than usual
- Changes in eating or sleeping habits
- Hints about suicide
- Loss of one or both parents because of death, divorce, or separation

Being aware of the warning signs that someone may be homeless will enable you to help a friend in need.

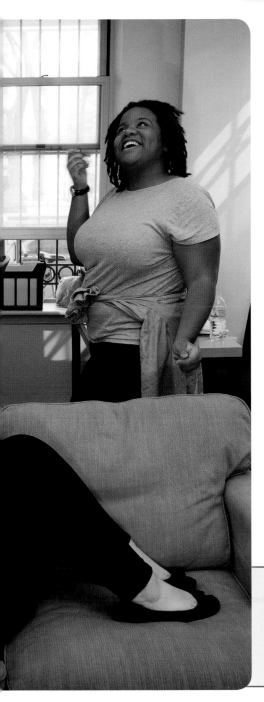

HOW TO TAKE ACTION BEFORE IT HAPPENS

If you think a friend is about to run away, you can talk to them before they leave. Offer them help in finding resources at school or in the community. It's always better to help someone before they become homeless than it is to help them later, when they may have lost some of the lifelines and safety nets to their previous life.

There are community resources, as well as helpful adults, who will try very hard to keep kids from running away. Start with your school principal or guidance

There are many people and places available to help homeless teens, especially before they become homeless and lose their lifelines.

counselor, who will be especially helpful if the friend you are worried about is one of their students.

They may be able to help the potential runaway find a temporary place to live or the professional help they need. And the same resources that are offered to homeless kids can also be used by concerned friends who want to help keep a friend off the streets.

If you aren't sure how to help, you can also ask your parents or a church or community resource. If you're worried that your friend is going to run away no matter what you try, then at least make sure that they have the phone number for the National Runaway Safeline (1-800-RUNAWAY). Then they will at least have a resource to use once the reality of being on the streets hits them.

Again another resource that should be shared with anyone thinking of running away or in danger of becoming homeless is the Safe Place program. By texting SAFE to 69866 or by looking for locations with a bright yellow triangle that says "Safe Place," a teen will be able to find safety, especially at times when they may be in danger of assault. Places with the Safe Place triangle, such as buses, will know the phone number to call to get help. Here is one story from Youthcare.org that serves as an example:

At 1:30 a.m. on December 31, 2011, seventeen-year-old Jared was out of options. His chaotic home life led him to realize that he could no longer stay with his family. He wandered, unsure of where to go. When he finally got on a King County Metro bus, the driver took one look at him and asked if he needed help. When Jared said "Yes," the driver knew what number to call. [A] Safe Place Coordinator took the call and met Jared downtown in the middle of the night. She came bearing her Safe Place kit —a blanket, a juice box, and granola bars. She has learned through experience that young people's basic survival needs must be met before even talking about shelter and safety. "He was wearing inadequate clothing for the weather, hadn't eaten in a while, and needed water," [the coordinator] said.

The Safe Place coordinator helped Jared find a place to stay in an emergency homeless shelter for teens, where he was also given the resources to find housing and return to school.

IF YOUR FRIEND IS A RUNAWAY

If all else fails and your friend does run away, what should you do? Kidshealth.org suggests:

If your friend does run away, or if you haven't seen him or her in a few days and you think that's what's happened, take action immediately. Talk to a trusted adult and explain that you believe your friend ran away. Don't be shy about sharing any information about where your friend might be

THE McKINNEY-VENTO ACT

Signed into law in 1987, the McKinney-Vento Act is a set of programs that provide services and assistance to the homeless. It has specific sections for homeless children and youth, defines exactly what criteria make a student homeless, and makes sure that they have immediate access to education. This includes transportation and the right to enroll even if they don't have the proper documents generally required for enrollment, such as a record of inoculations or vaccinations, or proof of residence. It also provides access to services that help homeless students. As reported by the official Washington State homepage, school districts are required to have a homeless liaison person, that is, an individual who makes sure that homeless youth are identified and then provided with the programs they need to succeed as students. School districts must also track their homeless students and report that data to the government. These measures are important, as homeless youth can easily slip through the cracks— missing out on an education that later will prove key to finding employment or other opportunities to excel in life.

going, and don't wait in hopes that he or she might come back after a few days. Your friend's life could depend on it — the sooner it is reported, the more likely your friend will be found safe.

It may not be easy to tell if a teen is homeless, even one who is a close friend. Many teens are embarrassed and ashamed of being homeless or afraid of being sent back into an abusive or violent situation at home, so they will hide it. Others may be homeless because their families have become homeless. The National Center for Homeless Education shares these warning signs that a teen might be homeless, including poor attendance at school, falling grades, reluctance to participate in after-school activities or social events, and changes in appearance such as wearing the same clothes or not being as well-groomed as before.

If a friend can't be talked out of running away, or admits to being homeless, the first thing that can be done, *with your parents' permission*, is offer to let them stay with you, even if it's just for a few nights. Remember, you might be tempted to hide your friend or pretend that it's just a regular sleepover, but you're not doing your friend any favors by keeping their presence a secret. But sometimes a "cooling off" period away from home can be what it takes for everyone to calm down. It also allows for some time to find alternatives to living at home, such as another relative to stay with or a shelter situation.

If your friend can't or won't contact any of the many local and national organizations that help runaways and homeless teens, you can call them yourself. Try to enlist the help of your parents or other trusted adults, but if your friend is adamant about not having any adult interference, you may have to do this on your own. Basically, you are trying to help your friend by giving them as much information as possible about resources and places to go for food and shelter.

You can also offer to be the contact address for your friend, so that mail can reach them. An address is often needed for anyone applying for a job, so this is something you can do to help your friend become employed. If you know where they will be and they don't have a cell phone, you can also offer to be their phone contact. If they do have a cell, you can be the one they check in with about where they are and how they're doing, and you can contact other people for them if necessary. Many homeless teens guard their whereabouts if they've left abusive homes, have broken the law, or simply don't want to be found. But you can be a neutral lifeline if necessary.

OTHER WAYS TO HELP THE HOMELESS

Even if you don't have a friend, classmate, or acquaintance who is homeless, you may still want to do something to help with the problem. The easiest way to do this is to volunteer with a shelter, hotline, or other organization that exists to help homeless teens. You might also volunteer to work at a soup kitchen, which gives you the opportunity to get to know the homeless teens in your area. There will be both local and national organizations for homeless teens that would welcome volunteers. Some of these include local YMCA or YWCA groups, Goodwill, or the Salvation Army. Local churches often have homeless outreach programs as well. Certain areas have their own organizations, such as Urban Street

Angels in San Diego, California. National organizations include Covenant House, Stand Up for Kids, and Volunteers of America. You can get started by googling "teen homeless resources" for your local area, or check out the websites for national organizations to see if there are links to local offices and opportunities for volunteering.

If you can't find an organization to volunteer with, you can also consider starting a homelessness project in your school, church, or community. It can be as simple as organizing a food or clothing drive for a local organization or starting an outreach resource for homeless teens where they can talk to another teen right in their school or community to help them find resources. It is best, however, to have an adult help organize your project and to be a mentor or sponsor (many schools require a faculty sponsor for clubs and activities anyway) to make sure that your efforts are appropriate and that no one is at risk, either the homeless students or the helping students.

Finally, you can also help on a very personal level by donating money and goods to homeless organizations if you don't have the time or ability to volunteer.

Most national organizations for homeless teens have websites where you can make a donation, and they ensure that your money goes to legitimate programs that help the homeless. It's also possible to help individual homeless teens that you may encounter on the street, but again, for your safety and theirs, it's best to be very careful. Some teens make up backpacks or bags of useful items like toiletries and snacks and give them out to homeless people on the streets. However, it's probably better to donate to existing homeless aid groups or shelters that know how to distribute money and goods to the people who need it the most and also know when someone is using homelessness as a scam to make money.

Nobody really wants to be homeless. But when you're a teen, it may seem like the only option for escaping a bad situation. Or it may be unavoidable, the result of bad economic times hitting your family. If you are homeless, or you know someone who is, there are many, many options and resources for you. Hopefully

One way to help the homeless in your area is to volunteer at a soup kitchen or shelter.

they can help you leave homelessness behind and lead the life you should. All it takes is some help and someone to believe in you. As one Covenant House director said about the teens he helps, "We put our arms around them, pat them on the back and dust them off. We feed them and we say, 'Despite what you've been through, tomorrow's a better day.'"

GLOSSARY

agency A business or organization that was created to serve a particular purpose, often for a transaction between groups of people.

alliance An organization that is formed for the mutual benefit of the people it serves.

deprivation The lack or denial of something that is considered to be a necessity.

episodic Something that happens occasionally and at irregular intervals of time.

evict To force someone to leave a property, often with the help of law enforcement officials.

frostbite Damage caused to body tissues by extreme cold, usually affecting the fingers, toes, and nose.

habitation A residence or a place to live, such as a house or apartment.

implication The conclusion that can be drawn from something, even if it isn't actually said.

initiative A new plan or process to achieve something or solve a problem.

lease A contract between a landlord and a tenant, with specific details about payments and terms.

liaison A person who helps organizations or groups to work together and provide information to each other.

obesity The condition of being extremely fat or overweight.

rehabilitation To bring someone back to a normal, healthy life after an illness, addiction, or crime.

resources A supply of money, materials, goods, or information that helps a person function effectively.

shelter A place that provides food and shelter to people such as the poor or homeless.

siblings Brothers and sisters with one or two parents in common.

subprime A mortgage or loan that is offered to borrowers with poor credit history, often at a very high interest rate.

substandard Something that is below the usual standard, usually of low quality, or is defective or inferior.

transitional Relating to a process or period of transition from one thing to another.

voucher A small piece of paper that can be exchanged for goods or services.

FOR MORE INFORMATION

Covenant House

Covenant House Headquarters
461 Eighth Avenue
New York, NY 10001
(800)-388-3888
Website: https://www.covenanthouse.org/about-
    homeless-charity/mission

*Covenant House is an organization for homeless and runaway teens
with houses located in twenty-seven cities in the United States,
Canada, and Latin America. Their mission is simply to help homeless
teens escape the streets.*

National Network for Youth

741 8th Street SE
Washington, DC 20003
(202) 783-7949
Website: https://www.nn4youth.org

*National Network for Youth is a national organization that provides
information about homelessness to government policymakers and the
general public.*

Raising the Roof

263 Eglinton Avenue West
Suite 200
Toronto, ON M4R 1B1
Canada
(416) 481-1838
Website: http://www.raisingtheroof.org

Raising the Roof is a national organization that works with local agencies across Canada to find long-term solutions to end homelessness

The Reciprocity Foundation
255 West 36th Street
Suite 1204
New York, NY 10018
(646) 692-4000
Website: http://www.reciprocityfoundation.org

The Reciprocity Foundation helps homeless, runaway, and foster care youth from all over New York City.

StandUp For Kids
83 Walton Street
Suite 500
Atlanta, GA 30303
(800)-365-4KID
Website: http://www.standupforkids.org

StandUp for Kids is a national charity that provides outreach services to homeless kids and teens. Volunteers, working mostly at night, bring food, clothing, and resource information to kids on the street.

True Colors Fund
330 West 38th Street
Suite 405
New York, NY 10018
(212) 461-4401
Website: https://truecolorsfund.org

The True Colors Fund works to end homelessness among lesbian, gay, transgender, and bisexual youth.

Youth Without Shelter
6 Warrendale Court
Toronto, ON M9V 1P9
Canada
(416) 748-0110
Website: http://www.yws.on.ca

Youth Without Shelter is an emergency shelter and referral service for Canadian teens in the Toronto area. They provide support services for homeless youth ages sixteen to twenty-four.

ROSENLINKS

Because of the changing nature of internet links, Rosen Publishing has developed an online list of websites related to the subject of this book. This site is updated regularly. Please use this link to access the list:

http://www.rosenlinks.com/411/home

FOR FURTHER READING

Berg, Ryan. *No House to Call My Home: Love, Family, and Other Transgressions.* New York, NY: Nation Books, 2015.

Desmond, Matthew. *Evicted: Poverty and Profit in the American City.* New York, NY: Crown Publishing, 2016.

Driver, Donald. *Driven: From Homeless to Hero: My Journeys On and Off Lambeau Field.* New York, NY: Three Rivers Press, 2014.

Edin, Kathryn J. *$2.00 a Day: Living on Almost Nothing in America.* New York, NY: Houghton Mifflin, 2015.

Gibson, Kristina E. *Street Kids: Homeless Youth, Outreach, and Policing New York's Streets.* New York, NY: NYU Press, 2011.

Gowan, Teresa. *Hobos, Hustlers, and Backsliders: Homeless in San Francisco.* Minneapolis, MN: University of Minnesota Press, 2010.

Hubbard, Jim. *Lives Turned Upside Down: Homeless Children in Their Own Words and Photographs.* New York, NY: Aladdin Books, 2007.

Irvine, Leslie. *My Dog Always Eats First: Homeless People and Their Animals.* Boulder, CO: Lynne Rienner Publishers, 2015.

Kennedy, Michelle. *Without a Net: Middle Class and Homeless (with Kids) in America.* New York, NY: Penguin Books, 2006.

Lowry, Kailin. *Pride Over Pity*. New York, NY: Post Hill Press, 2014.

Murray, Liz. *Breaking Night: A Memoir of Forgiveness, Survival, and My Journey from Homeless to Harvard*. New York, NY: Hachette Books, 2011.

Padgett, Deborah. *Housing First: Ending Homelessness, Transforming Systems, and Changing Lives*. New York, NY: Oxford University Press, 2015.

Ross, Anthony D. *Homeless at Age 13 to a College Graduate: An Autobiography*. Manila, Philippines: Step One Publishing, 2014.

Ryan, Kevin and Tina Kelley. *Almost Home: Helping Kids Move from Homelessness to Hope*. New York, NY: Wiley, 2012.

Seider, Scott. Shelter: *Where Harvard Meets the Homeless*. New York, NY: Bloomsbury Academic, 2010.

Sweeney, Bob. *Homeless No More: A Solution for Families, Veterans, and Shelters*. Dallas, TX: Dallas LIFE, 2015.

Van Draanen, Wendelen. *Runaway*. New York, NY: Ember Publishing, 2012.

Wasserman, Jason Adam. *At Home on the Street: People, Poverty, and a Hidden Culture of Homelessness*. Boulder, CO: Lynne Rienner Publishers, 2009.

Wayne, Jimmy. *Walk to Beautiful: The Power of Love and a Homeless Kid Who Found the Way*. Nashville, TN: Thomas Nelson, 2015.

BIBLIOGRAPHY

"A Message to Homeless Teens." Survival Guide to Homelessness. December 6, 2004. Web. http://www .guide2homelessness.blogspot.com/2004/04/12/ message-to-homeless-teens.html

Briscoe, Tony. "Survey Tries to Shed Light on Hidden Homeless Youths." *Chicago Tribune*, September 9, 2015. http://www.chicagotribune.com/news/ct-chicago -homeless-youth-met-20150909-story.html.

"Consequences of Youth Homelessness." National Net-work for Youth. Web. Accessed July 1, 2016. https:// www.nn4youth.org/wp-content/uploads/IssueBrief _Youth_Homelessness.pdf

Daniels, David G. "The Race of My Life: A Runaway Kid's Story." Children's Rights blog, May 15, 2015. http://www.childrensrights.org/the-race-of-my-life-a -runaway-kids-story/.

Desmond, Matthew. *Evicted: Poverty and Profit in the American City*. New York, NY: Crown Publishers, 2016.

"Don't Call Them Dropouts: Understanding the Experiences of Young People Who Leave High School Before Graduation." Tufts University, America's

Promise Alliance, 2014. http://www.gradnation.org/
sites/default/files/DCTD percent20Final percent20Full
.pdf.

"Education of Homeless Children and Youth." State of
Washington. Accessed April 4, 2016. http://www.k12
.wa.us/HomelessEd/AssistanceAct.aspx.

"Family Homelessness Facts." Green Doors. Accessed
April 2, 2016. http://www.greendoors.org/facts/family
-homelessness.php.

"Fact Sheet: Why Are People Homeless?" National
Coalition for the Homeless, July 2009. http://www
.nationalhomeless.org/factsheets/why.html.

"Federal Definitions," Youth.gov. Accessed April 2, 2016.
http://youth.gov/youth-topics/runaway-and-homeless
-youth/federal-definitions.

"General Homelessness Facts." Green Doors. Accessed
April 2, 2016. http://www.greendoors.org/facts/general
-data.php.

"Homeless Youth: Defining the Problem and the
Population." National Resource Center on Domestic
Violence. Accessed April 2, 2016. http://www.nrcdv.org/
rhydvtoolkit/each-field/homeless-youth/define.html.

Horvath, Mark. "My First Night Homeless: A True
Story." Huffpost Impact, June 20, 2011. http://www
.huffingtonpost.com/mark-horvath/my-first-night
-homeless_b_850145.html.

"HUD Exchange: Resources for Homeless Youth." U.S. Department of Housing and Urban Development. Accessed April 3, 2016. https://www.hudexchange .info/homelessness-assistance/resources-for-homeless -youth/.

"I Couldn't Imagine Doing This Every Day." Covenant House News, March 28, 2016. https://www .covenanthouse.org/homeless-youth-news/i-couldnt -imagine-doing-every-day.

James, Charley. "Double Trouble for Homeless Teens." Daily Kos, July 18, 2012. http://www.dailykos.com/ story/2012/7/18/1111383/-Suddenly-Homeless-20 -Double-Trouble-For-Homeless-Teens.

"Jared: Metro Bus Leads to Safety." Youthcare. Accessed April 4, 2016. http://www.youthcare.org/youth-stories -jared#.VwJp7EdG5WA.

"Jodie's Story: A Life Full of Promise." Covenant House. Accessed April 2, 2016. https://www.covenanthouse .org/homeless-kids/life-full-promise.

"Karen's Story: Alone in the Cold." Covenant House. Accessed April 2, 2016. https://www.covenanthouse .org/homeless-kids/alone-cold.

"Kathy's Story: This Belongs to Me." Covenant House. Accessed April 2, 2016. https://www.covenanthouse .org/homeless-kids/belongs-me.

"LGBTQ HOMELESS YOUTH FACT SHEET." National Alliance to End Homelessness. Accessed April 2, 2016. http://www.safeschoolscoalition.org/LGBTQhomelessFactSheetbyNAEH.pdf.

"My Friend Is Talking About Running Away. What Should I Do?" Teenhealth.com. The Nemours Foundation. Accessed April 4, 2016. http://kidshealth .org/en/teens/runaway.html.

"NN4Y Issue Brief: Consequences of Youth Homelessness." National Network for Youth. Accessed April 3, 2016. https://www.nn4youth.org/wp-content/uploads/IssueBrief_YouthHomelessness .pdf.

Pannoni, Alexandra, "Homeless High Schoolers Face Barriers to Education." U.S. News & World Report, September 29, 2014. Web. http://www.usnews.com/education/blogs/high-school-notes/2014/09/29/homeless-high-schoolers-face-barriers-to-education.

"Potential Warning Signs of Homelessness." National Center for Homeless Education. Web. Accessed July 5, 2016. http://center/serve/org/nche/nche/warning.html

"Poverty: 2014 Highlights." U.S. Census Bureau. Web. Accessed April 2, 2016. https://www.census.gov/hhes/www/poverty/about/overview/.

Quigley, Bill, and Sara H. Godchaux. "Locked Out and Torn Down: Public Housing Post Katrina." Bill

Quigley Social Justice Advocacy blog. Accessed April 2, 2016. https://billquigley.wordpress.com/2015/06/08/locked-out-and-torn-down-public-housing-post-katrina-by-bill-quigley-and-sara-h-godchaux/.

Romero, Farida Jhabvala. "Teen Health Van Delivers More Than Medical Care To Homeless Youth." National Public Radio, February 17, 2016. http://www.npr.org/sections/health-shots/2016/02/17/466945298/teen-health-van-delivers-more-than-medical-care-to-homeless-youth.

Ruf, Cory. "Hamilton's Homeless Youth Face Mental Health Challenges." CBC, October 24, 2012. http://www.cbc.ca/news/canada/hamilton/news/hamilton-s-homeless-youth-face-mental-health-challenges-1.1204041.

"Runaways." Miami Museum of Science. Accessed April 4, 2016. http://www.miamisci.org/youth/unity/Unity1/Rosena/pages/index.html.

Slesnick, Dr. Natasha. "The Forgotten Children: Unaccompanied Runaway and Homeless Youth." Ohio State University. Accessed April 3 2016. http://ccec.ehe.osu.edu/files/2014/09/Whitepaper_Summer_14-04SEP2014_FINAL.pdf.

"State of Homelessness in America 2015." National Alliance to End Homelessness, April 1, 2015. http://www.endhomelessness.org/library/entry/the-state-of-homelessness-in-america-2015.

"Teen Homelessness Statistics." Covenant House. Accessed April 2, 2016. https://www.covenanthouse .org/homeless-teen-issues/statistics.

"Three LGBT Youths Describe Being Homeless in NYC." *Advocate*, December 21, 2015. http://www.advocate .com/commentary/2015/12/21/three-lgbt-youths -describe-being-homeless-nyc.

"Trauma Among Homeless Youth." Culture and Trauma Brief, The National Child Traumatic Stress Network, V2 n1 2007. http://www.nctsnet.org/nctsn_assets/pdfs/ culture_and_trauma_brief_v2n1HomelessYouth.pdf.

Tucker, McKenna. "Rail Riders: Teens Turn Hobo in a Crumbling Country." iGlobe. Accessed April 2, 2016. http://www.icademyglobe.org/article.php?id=687.

"Understanding the Health Care Needs of Homeless Youth." HRSA Health Service Program. Web. Accessed July 1, 2016. http://bphc.hrsa.gov/archive/ policiesregulations/policies/pal200110.html

"Understanding the McKinney-Vento Homeless Assistance Act of 2001." Family and Youth Services Bureau. Web. Accessed July 1, 2016. http://ncfy.acf .hhs.gov/features/opening-school-doors-runaway -and-homeless-youth/understanding-mickinney- vento-homeless

Wender, Samantha, and Geoff Martz. "Nowhere to Go, Teen Lived in Tree." ABC News, January 28, 2011. http://abcnews.go.com/US/teens-trouble-homeless

-youth-lived-tree/story?id=12779365.

"What To Do When You're Homeless—The Ultimate Guide." Venture Articles. Accessed April 3, 2016. http://www.venturearticles.com/what-to-do-when -youre-homeless.html.

"Why Do Young People Become Homeless?" The Homeless Hub. Web. Accessed July 1, 2016. http:// homelesshub.ca/resource/why-do-young-people -become-homeless

INDEX

ABOUT THE AUTHOR

Marcia Amidon Lusted is the author of numerous books and magazine articles for young readers. She has also worked as a teacher, a bookseller, and a magazine editor. She is a writer and editor for adults, as well as a musician and permaculturist. In her travels to cities around the United States and overseas, she has seen many homeless children, teens, and adults firsthand. You can find out more about her at www.adventuresinnonfiction.com.

PHOTO CREDITS

Cover, p. 1 SpeedKingz/Shutterstock.com; p. 5 Spencer Platt/ Getty Images News/Getty Images; pp. 6–7 © iStockphoto .com/Steve Debenport; pp. 10–11 Bettmann/Getty Images; pp. 12–13, 14–15 John Moore/Getty Images News/Getty Images; pp. 16–17 © John Birdsall/The Image Works; pp. 22–23, 82–83 The Washington Post/Getty Images; pp. 24–25 FEMA/Jocelyn Augustino; pp. 26–27 Maxal Tamor/ Shutterstock.com; pp. 30–31 Joe Raedle/Getty Images; pp. 34–35 Kevin Cooley/Stone/Getty Images; pp. 42–43 Richard Heinzen/SuperStock; pp. 44–45 © Socialstock/TopFoto/The Image Works; pp. 46–47 AP Images for Samsung; pp. 50–51 © iStockphoto.com/Andrea Zanchi; pp. 52–53 Monkey Business Images/Shutterstock.com; pp. 56–57 © iStockphoto .com/Arthur Carlo Franco; pp. 58–59 Kathryn Scott Osler/ The Denver Post/Getty Images; pp. 64–65 © iStockphoto .com//Todor Tsvetkov; pp. 66–67 Tim Boyle/Getty Images;

Designer: Les Kanturek; Editor: Rachel Gluckstern; Photo Researcher: Nicole DiMella